KIRBY PETERMAN

SUNFLOWERS

To my family, because without you all, I would still think
ants have no arms or legs.

To my parents for loving me even when I did not understand
what that meant.

And to my grandfather, who I wish could have seen me share my voice.

Not till we are lost, in other words not till we have lost the world, do we begin to find ourselves, and realize where we are and the infinite extent of our relations.

HENRY DAVID THOREAU

Contents

Contents

A NOTE TO YOU FROM ME-

Continuing to live after trauma requires daily effort. Through writing with complete transparency, I have found solace in understanding where my own trauma now fits into my story. The outcome is a journey through my life and a deeper understanding of who I am because of, and in spite of, my experiences. I learned to recognize my growth in a way I had never let myself when I tried to forget my past.

I do not know where I am headed in life. I've learned that this is not a feeling unique to me and have gained comfort in the limitlessness provided by this ambiguity. Still, the understanding of myself is a gradual one, developing through and sometimes against time. We are born with our bodies, but we must discover our souls.

Unfortunately, in today's society in which women strive to gain their own foundation but are often stifled by expectations of their sexuality, of their bodies, of their emotions, it is increasingly difficult to discover one's self. In this world of political facades, discrimination, materialism, and inequality, transparency can be dangerous. My vulnerability in this piece is given to you, the reader, with the intention to provoke your own associations and to promote conversation about our society.

Growing up, I was conditioned to internally deal with my feelings, to swallow my words, and mute my emotions. This was normal and became unquestionably easy. Getting older, and encountering experiences with greater weight, challenged this silent coping mechanism, so I learned to write. I believe as humans it is a worthwhile endeavor to share the very experiences you may try to forget in an effort to push beyond them and pull up others who may be wrestling their own stories. This is not our duty, however, and should be taken at a healthy pace.

My grandfather, Leonard Robbins, was a man who was essential in the racial integration in public schools of Houston, Texas and who was instrumental in allowing women to even wear pants to school. A story I have often heard of him was of a time he spoke about his schoolboard work and my mother, his daughter, watched as he was slapped on live television. Of course, this did not stop him, instead he was provided with one of the first car telephones by police and pushed forward. Not only was he dedicated to the story of future generations, but he devoted most of his post-retirement life to creating books of our family's genealogy. In the books, I am lucky to find the voice of my ancestors - their stories, their relations, the source of my middle names, the people whose lives led to my own.

After he passed, I was able to receive printed compilation made up of years of his poetry in which he writes of his mental health, of his schoolboard work, of his children. While I always had viewed him as a stoic, quiet grandfather, I see now that he had a mighty voice that comforts me beyond his time on Earth.

A few years before he passed, he pulled me aside and said, "I know it is a pain in the ass, but you should share your voice. I am the same as you, but it is worth it to speak". I took it at my own pace, but I understand now.

-Kirby

I'll climb out the window
my bare feet on the grass
and then I'll run
out of this place
out of my head
out of breath
and I'll fall
onto the dirt
over my toes
into the arms
of what's to come

-my skinned knees burning and all

SUNFLOWERS

KIRBY PETERMAN

Intellectual Soulmate

You will stop at a red light with your best friend in your junior year of high school. Liz and you will not be good at sharing emotions with anyone except each other. It will be a summer day in Houston so your windows will be down but the air conditioner in your car will be on. Wasteful but comfortable. Driving is your favorite activity with Liz. The freedom of the roads, the endless conversation, the music discoveries. These drives will sustain your friendship.

Later in your life, you will miss these drives like a piece of yourself.

"Wanna cruise?" She will have texted you earlier that day. Of course you wanted to. You had already told your mom you were leaving to do homework and were down your street before you texted her back that you were on your way. Liz knows more than you about a lot of things - calculus, boys, sex, drinking, clothes, saving money. She has the healthiest hair of anyone you know; dark brown with natural lighter strands that can be thrown into a ponytail and still be elegant. Freckles shine all over her face; a mask of youthfulness that she sometimes dislikes but you often envy. The way she carries herself is feminine yet effortless. She can throw parties on Fridays and spend a day with you in an art museum on Saturday.

Still, sometimes she will be dark within herself. You will write her letters for every occasion trying to explain how meaningful her existence will always be. Years later, you will send similar words in cards even though you will not live near each other.

Now, however, you have have both decided to swear off men for the rest of high school.

Bastards! You call them. She is an incomparable listener and your advice guru on these drives. Both of you quit therapy together. Nothing worse could exist than being vulnerable with someone else.

"One day you will find a guy who is just as intelligent as you. He will understand your soul. You will go on long drives with him and talk about life and smoke weed and listen to good music and it will feel effortless. He will be the right guy."

She told you this at the stop light. Too much emotion being directed at you starts to give you that heavy sense of dissonance between the guilt and relief of talking about yourself, so you laugh instead of responding. You have never been good at receiving or expressing emotion.

You will change the subject, but never forget.

TWO

Plastic Peas

As the youngest sister, you will be the child in your imaginary world with your sisters that unfolds within your playroom. You're five years old. Katharyn, the boy this year, is your father. Sara, the girl this year, is the mother. Mostly, you sit out. You have been playing 'Family' with your sisters all afternoon. Katharyn goes to work in the corner and pretends to dial and talk on the Barbie phone. Sara stays home. "I'm your teacher at school now," Sara switches roles to be your teacher and grabs a folder for your homework. She talks about addition until you declare the school bell has rung. She is your mother again and starts making dinner. Plastic pizzas, plastic peas, even a plastic kitchen. When Katharyn gets off of work five minutes later, she comes home to her wife. "We kiss each other but let's not actually do it," Katharyn declares. She says hi to you, their child. It is bed time now, you sit out again. They have a date night over their plastic meal and declare their love for each other.

You could play Family all day. This time you are a young child but maybe later you will be a moody teenager or a son who sags his pants. Maybe you will be the smartest kid in the world and your play parents will praise your brilliance.

Your mom will call you all to dinner and your Family will dissipate. You ask if your sisters will keep playing after you eat and you persist with constant begging after they say no. Why would they give up on your Family? The utmost betrayal – you decide you won't speak for the rest of dinner.

THREE

Turbulence

You will wake up in the middle of the night, thirsty for water. The darkness will make you feel alone. Instead, however, you will see your father on the couch. He is sleeping with a pillow and a blanket from his bed that he should be sharing with your mother. You will freeze on the stairs as a wave of something you don't understand makes you feel heavy – like the shock of airplane turbulence that makes your stomach tug on your heart. You step softly back up the stairs. You don't feel thirsty anymore but your stomach hurts so you curl up and try to sleep.

Your brain disobeys, beginning to piece together the story as excerpts of your parents' prior bickering resonate through your body.

Intrusive. Guilty.

Your mind dives deep into its fabrication, trying to make you choose which parent you will live with if they split. You will squeeze your eyes until your face is fatigued and fall asleep trying to decide which stuffed animal you would keep at each of their houses.

FOUR

Longing

Walking back from the grocery store with your mother you will talk about your friend, Ryan's, parents getting a divorce. Her mother has moved out of your neighborhood and she now lives with only her dad. Cars speed past on the busy road drowning out your soft voice and you wait to repeat yourself until there is a break in traffic.

Ryan had told you while waiting outside your classroom the week before. You did not know how to console her and you felt wrong to ask her what it meant for them to be divorced. Where was she going to live and did her parents ever talk to each other? Was she going to keep her dog? Could you still go to her house?

"I hope daddy and I do not ever get to that point," is all your mother has to say and she puts her hand out for you to hold. You look up to her, but she only stares into the distance ahead. She looks as if she is longing for something, but you're too young and inexperienced to know.

Now you'll know, it is affection she longs for.

First Kiss

It is first grade and you have met the love of your life, Andres. As your class lines up for lunch, he will pull you out of line even though he knows you love being line leader. Following him into the sink room that connects your classroom with the neighboring class, he will quickly look at you and smile. Standing, face to face, he will kiss you. Then you will both squeal, wipe your lips with the backs of your hands, swish water in your mouths, and run back into line.

Later, at lunch, you will eavesdrop on him finally being initiated into The Boy's Club at the end of the lunch table because he has kissed a girl. You will throw up your lunch and go to the nurse.

A kiss. A heart break.

At home, you will feel guilty, ashamed, and quiet. In the shower you will cry and try to scrub your lips.

Naive

Hearing your sister, Katharyn, crying your name through intermittent sobs from her room, you will find her, leaning over her bed, her face swollen. She knows her boyfriend is going to break up with her. You have never had a real boyfriend and cannot understand how she knows.

"Look at the way he is talking to me, I know what this means." She shows you her texts from him.

You hug her, vowing to yourself that you will never date anyone who will break up with you, deciding you will stay single until you find your true love.

Just Not Today

Sitting on the floor of your dorm room, you will hang up the phone. Alone. Despair.

Swollen eyelids. Denial. What just happened? Quinn has broken up with you. You're too sad. He cannot see a future with someone who cannot see a future in herself. He cannot deal with long distance anymore and he feels bad for not knowing how to be a better boyfriend. He doesn't know why he is doing this. You will look up at the pictures of you and Quinn smothering your wall. The smiles that once made you warm now mock you. Laugh at you. You will skip class and fill your bed with tissues. You will miss your best friend Liz and wish you went to the same college. You will call your mom. You will wash your sheets. You will vow to take down all the pictures and take off the bracelet and necklace he gave you tomorrow.

Just not today.

EIGHT

Breakup Soup

You'll think back to high school when Aiden invited you over. You had lost good friends for him and you found yourself going to his house every day to compensate. You were only together a few months and you were still nervous about the physicality he expected from you so quickly. Shirt off, on the couch, he sat up and asked you if you were trying to actually date and told you he did not want to really be together. You coolly said you didn't want to date either as if he had just cracked a bad joke. Then you tried to convince yourself of this. You took deep breaths trying not to turn too red. You started to notice each spot on your stomach that folded over on itself. You hugged yourself, hiding the flaws that must be disgusting him. You went to the bathroom, rubbing your nose in the mirror. Maybe it is too big for him, you had thought. You felt embarrassed of your unruly hair and attempted an attractive messy bun until your arms got tired and tingly. Instead of perfectly loose pieces framing your face, you looked like man who forgot to trim your sideburns. The space behind your eyes heated up and sent pressure to the front of your throat until you told yourself you were ridiculous to cry. You wanted to go home but you walked downstairs and ate dinner with his parents and brothers. Stirring your spoon in your miso soup, taking a few forced bites, helping with dishes.

Outside, he kissed you and said he did not know how to be with someone so sad. You walked home in the darkness. Sad. Relieved.

NINE

Celestial Acceptance

He is not the sun

And you are not the earth

You are the stars, honey
You are the space, in between
You are the gravity, pulling into orbit
You are the edges, expanding into infinity

So no,
He is not the sun
He is a comet burning in your atmosphere

Making his way out

Melancholy Waves

The first time you spend a week in bed you will feel lazy, a burden even. Guilty about your laziness. Too tired to change. Too hazy. You will be too empty to get up yet too sad to stay alone. You will not sleep. You will sleep too much. You will feel stuck, weighed down by the dense pull of your own brain. Your thoughts will tell you that you are scared of what is happening, but your soul will feel as close to nothing as humanly possible. You will not love what you thought you loved. Reading will feel boring. The sun, too bright. Your family, too imposing. Your friends, too demanding. It will be summer break and you will be precisely half way through high school and still not care. You will hardly remember the past two years and only feel comfortable in the darkness of your room, the humidity of your unclean sheets, and the silence of your solitude.

"I do not feel well, I'm just not hungry," you will convince your parents. But you will waste away, comfortably.

The white ceiling above will fulfill your entertainment needs. Your cat will lick your tears and you will let him, even though his tongue hurts. The skin on your friends' bodies will grow bronzer, their muscles toner. Your skin will grow whiter than your sheets and looser than your oversized clothes.

And then, after some time, you will drag yourself out from between your sheets and into the shower.

After a while, you will clean your entire room vigorously and scrub your body in the warmth of the shower, only to wonder what had happened that provided you with so much energy again.

You are not a burden.
    It will happen again, and you will still not be a burden.

ELEVEN

Invisible Wilting

When you are sixteen, wearing furry animal ears and a short black skater dress on Halloween, you'll tell everyone you are a cat. You will be laughing on the ground, having fallen in the middle of a neighborhood street with too much vodka tracing through your veins and just enough weed blackening your lungs to make you feel carefree. Your friends will call Blake, who you have never spoken to before, to pick you all up and you will feel thankful. He will drive you to a party and your friends will get out as his hands wrap around your waist to keep you inside. "I didn't know you drank," he will say to you and then you will be in the backseat, straddled around him, trusting his arms to keep you upright. You'll have sex for the first time. It will be quick, passionless, and you will be too intoxicated for it to be memorable – except for the end when he tells you to go back to the party and the blood you find on your thighs in the morning.

And he does not know me but I let him touch me

And our tongues are supposed to dance but his takes over

And our bodies are supposed to feel like one but I feel invisible

TWELVE

Libra Resilience

You will take an art history class your senior year of high school with Annie. In your wealthy Texas high school, she defends her liberal beliefs with unwavering confidence despite the unpopularity. She expresses herself through clothes and style, she ignores the social boundaries of cliques that occur in high school, she shows you how to speak your mind, and maybe most importantly, how to cover your hands in doodles when you're bored. No one will make you laugh as heartily as Annie. At her house when you sleep over in middle school you will laugh so hard with her at night that her parents will have to tell you to go to sleep. When you both finally get your driver's licenses you will proceed to drive aimlessly, listening to Sugarhill Gang's *Rapper's Delight* for an entire day after deciding it would be an impressive party trick to turn on the song and break out into a smooth, unerring rap. You still will not get past the first stanza but you will know those lines for life. Annie will show you how to embrace your womanhood, how to be independent, and how to appreciate the power of humor.

In art history, Mrs. June will embody the dangerous beliefs associated with the stereotype of the American South.

"If my son raped a girl and she was wearing slutty clothing he should not go to jail and he should not be blamed," Mrs. June will say several times throughout the semester, continuing to explain that it should be the girl's fault for being a slut.

Annie will stand up in class each time and tell Mrs. June how wrong she is. She will fight Mrs. June's racism, her sexism, her discrimination.

No one else will say anything, not even you.

Other days Mrs. June will ask the one student with brown skin to "explain what the Muslim religion is," and upon his lack of knowledge, she will ask him how he expects Americans to learn about his religion if he cannot even explain it. She will declare that college is all about partying. She will tell the class that her husband is a "butt man". She will pop blood vessels in her feet from stomping too hard as she runs out of defense for her ignorance against Annie. Her wrinkled skin will redden and tremble with her misinformed irritation. You and Annie will decide she is the spawn of Satan.

You will want to squeeze love into Annie for her boldness and you will think about it for the rest of your life. Her flushed cheeks. Her confidence. Her strong voice. Her resilience. Her pride in femininity and passion for equality.

The summer after your first year of college, you will go back to Houston and drive around with Annie. She will be the first person outside of your family that you ever tell about your assault and she will tell you a terrifying experience of her own.

At home, later, you will cry. You will cry about the world you live in and feel alien. You will become frustrated, then angry. You will feel hatred and you will feel helpless. How could a woman as powerful as Annie ever be made to feel so powerless? Why?

It will be the first time you think sharing your voice could be important and you will decide in the future you might write it all down.

THIRTEEN

Voiceless

Standing in a crowd at a music festival, you will dance in front of your boyfriend. He will ride his hands up your outer leg. The group in front of you starts jumping. Your friends will start screaming. He is fumbling. Up your shorts. You will just want to dance and decide to hold his hand if he gets too far. You should let him have a little fun, you will think. You will look down but it is a different hand. Your boyfriend's body will start jumping behind you, his hands in the air above your head, following the beat of the song. You will trace the arm. It is the boy next to you, dancing with another girl. Into you. Grimy. You feel grimy. The whole crowd starts shifting, the music gets louder. You look at him but he is kissing the neck of the other girl. The person in front of you jumps and lands on your feet. His fingers start to move within you. It stings. Speak. Speak! You cannot speak. You will squirm. Moving away, you will tell your boyfriend. He will ask why you did not say something earlier.

FOURTEEN

Tonic Immobility

"Get your shoes and get out," he will tell you after he rapes you.
You are eighteen. Your clothes never came off. You never touched
him back when it got too far. You did not cry for help either.

He covered the window with a pillow after locking the door. He
smiled down at you. You will regret going to the fraternity party with
your friends. You did not want to go. Why did you not cry for help?
What just happened? You will run down the stairs past others but
you will not be able to release more than a whimper. You will run
hysterically. 14th Street? An alley? Where are you? What happened?
He pinned you down. Why did you not push him off of you? You will
call Quinn but he is in Texas so he will call the police. Sirens. 15th
street? Behind a trash can you will hide. Hide from the sirens, hide
from what just happened. What just happened? You were sober. You
will wish you were not. "Honey, if you don't report him you might

let this happen to other girls." You will spend six more hours in an emergency room. Rape kit. Apple juice. They will take your favorite thong. Alone you will wait. Driven back to your dorm in a police car, you will tell everyone you are fine. What just happened? You will not tell your parents. You will not tell your sister. You will not file a case against him. You will ask to never know his name. "Don't let this happen to someone else, you need to file a case." Why did you go to the party? Why did you not cry for help? What was his name? Why did you not push him off of you?

FIFTEEN

Shriveling

Quinn will visit you a week after the assault. He will get on top of you and you will panic. He will ask you if it is okay and you will just nod. You will not want it to not be okay.

Shivers. Tears. Suffocating.

It is happening again. What is happening? You will go outside in shorts even though it is cold and windy and you will cry. Cry for your past self. Cry for your future self. Cry so hard that you continue to gasp after your tears have run out.

SIXTEEN

It Is Not Your Fault, It Is Not My Fault

"You should not have put yourself in that situation" your parents will tell you on the phone when they get the emergency room bill.

I should not have put myself in that situation. Why did I not cry for help?

It is not your fault.
 It is not my fault.

You will lie.
You will tell them you got away from him. They are terrified too.

Your sister will be with you and she will hang up on them.

SEVENTEEN

It Is Not Your Fault, Baby Girl

Sleeping will lose its charm. Nightmares. Flashbacks. You will call Janice instead. She was your nanny until you were 15. She raised you in her cushioned hugs and her mischievous nature, teaching you affection, showing you to take life lightly. She will know what to tell you. She was raped too, when she was 14, you will learn.

Maybe the dark times will always be with you, she will tell you, but they will become distant.

It is not your fault, baby girl, you will only grow stronger.

EIGHTEEN

Innocence

You will turn six and your mother will tell you Nicholas, whose birthday is near yours, has called you on the phone asking you to sleep over. You will nervously say yes. You love his soft ear lobes even though everyone will laugh when you say so. You will overhear your mother say you are close to the age when boys and girls cannot sleep over anymore.

NINETEEN

Triggers

It is your first party of the year in your new apartment with your three roommates. You will invite your boyfriend Eli over. He will get drunk. You will get into bed. Exhausted. Socially exhausted. You will tell Eli to go home. He will take off his pants and get into bed

Uncomfortable, you'll sneak your body as far toward the edge of the bed as you can. You will sit up and you will stiffen. You'll tell him to leave again.

Uncomfortable.

I am uncomfortable.

You're making me uncomfortable.

He will tell you he is not leaving.

Why did I not cry for help?
Why did I not push him off of me?

You will push Eli out of the bed. He will yell. He will tell you he is going to fucking kill himself because of you. Flying across the kitchen he will kick your trash can. He will drive off, drunk.

Why did I push him off of me?

TWENTY

A Cold Apology

I'm sorry about what I did last night, Wyatt will message you. Your first party since moving to college, classes have not started yet so you follow your new friends to parties. He will lock you in a bathroom and you will do what he tells you with his pants down and your knees on the cold ground, just so that he will unlock the door.

You will swear off men for all of college. You swear.

TWENTY ONE

Regrowth

You will be two miles into a hike with your best friend, Clayton. Your journey began on an early morning in that cusp between winter and spring when you feel lucky to finally bathe in a sunny morning again but you can still feel the tension between the seasons that arises as the solstice draws closer. You approach a bridge over running snow melt. The sun glistens down on the water, reflecting beams into the canyon wall next to you and onto your skin. Following the sound of crashing water, you will discover a waterfall. The collision of water on water sends droplets flying against your faces.

You will remember two summers prior feeling the dense beat of your heart as it was hitting your sternum, trying to keep you alive long enough to take a shower. The water scorched your skin in that disturbingly comfortable way that you might keep squeezing blood out of a paper cut. You had looked down and watched your heart's rhythm in your stomach, drumming under the path of the water droplets that had not dissipated into steam. Steam that seemed to weigh down your lungs. Your arms depended on the shower wall to keep your body upright. You had closed your eyes, taken your deepest breath, and plunged your face into the shower water, hoping to waste as much time, as much water, scrub off enough skin cells, become dizzy enough, to drown the growls of your suffering body. You reached up to turn the water one nudge hotter. Your toes red, your heart ever-pounding. You had passed out in the shower that day, only for a few minutes. No one knew except you. You were too thin and denied it.

Now, as the cold water sprinkles your face, you will want more of it, you will want to jump in it, splash, leap. To feel your place in the world as a living being. You hiked here. Two years after being unable to stand long enough to clean your body.

"Your body is what takes you on adventures. Food fuels your body to let you experience life." Your sister had desperately tried to get this idea through the blockade in your brain. But anorexia is a self-sufficient beast. You had convinced yourself that life was not an adventure with you here in the world.

You had withered away. It was a long time coming. Your skin draped along your cheekbones and deep into the joints of your wrists and shoulders. Your ribs and hips created valleys under your shirt when you laid in bed. You were too tired to cry. Too dark to laugh. Too afraid to tell anyone for so long. Long enough that it was imperative you be admitted to the hospital several times. Cue the electrodes on your chest to watch your heart. The calorie tracking. No more yoga. No more running. No more freedom to choose your own meals.

Vitamin supplements, electrolyte-filled drinks, talk about your feelings once a week.

You will hear the sound of Clayton praising you for regaining your health. The feeling of the breeze congratulating you. In the future, Clayton will still praise you as you get healthier. He will be your best friend for life as well as your cheerleader. He will make you laugh and he will be your voice when you cannot be your own. He will make you realize the importance of friendship. He will show you that men can advocate for women too.

Anorexia is a self-sufficient beast
but the power within is strong enough to overcome it.

Embodiment

My body is a sanctuary of possibility.

I am alive as birds are alive.

I breathe the air of the trees.

I experience the change of the seasons

and am shaded by the same clouds that shade
the mountains surrounding me.

Who Are You?

You will swear off men.
Swear off men so hard you will decide to date yourself.

Who are you?

In A Relationship With Myself

"I love your crazy hair in the morning," I whispered to Her.

She looked at me – her eyelids batting slowly under the weight of the
new sun. Her curls defied gravity, spinning upwards
as if they had been caught within the wildness of her dreams at night.

I convinced her to watch the sunrise with me,
We brought coffee out to the edge of our roof –
      vowing to replace the window screen We had to rip off before
      our landlord noticed –

The eastern clouds beckoned the sun,
mimicking its early pinkness until it surpassed their height

and We could finally uncurl our legs out of our shirts under the emergent warmth.

We followed the comfort into Our bath
Stretching Our legs through the lavender salts as Our muscles slackened,

I slipped my hands along Her thighs
Outward, then inward
Her skin, pulpy silk under the water, inviting Me further.

The water cooled and We toweled off.

"I'll be with You forever." She spoke to Me with the calmness that accompanies truth.

 I laughed, looking at my reflection,

The pudge of my stomach
The jiggle of my arms
My lack of eyelashes
Misshapen brows

All beautiful, like my own tiger stripes unique to me,

And she stared back at me,
On the other side of the mirror – my reflection.
"I've wanted you to love me back all along," She smiled, relieved.

He Does Not Represent Men

It was not your fault, your therapist will tell you.
  It was never your fault.

You did not ask for that to happen.
  You could not have prevented it either.

He does not represent men.

Self-Love and Sunflowers

You will meet Bella in psychological statistics. You will sit in the front row together. She will teach you self-love. She will teach you true friendship. She will show you that it was not your fault. She will help you understand your parents were just scared and did not know what to say. She will see how much they love you before you do. She will love you when you cannot love yourself. She will be in tune with you even when you push her away and she will love you harder when you let her back in. You will understand why owls are her spirit animal. She will be your best friend and she will tell you that and you will believe her.

"You're a sunflower," she will tell you, but it will take you time to accept that.

TWENTY SEVEN

Nurture

What flower is she?" Bella will ask Sam about you.

"A sunflower," he will declare.

"Did you know sunflowers absorb radiation and grow into beautiful flowers? They have a dark center but a strong stem and they turn with the sun."

Yellow will become your favorite color.

You learn that sunflowers follow the Golden Ratio, their petals spiraling in Fibonacci numbers, manifested through a genome larger than that of humans.

In actuality, only young sunflowers track the sun.

As they mature and strengthen,
they find a fixed easterly stance to face the rising sun.

TWENTY EIGHT

He Does Represent Men

His happiness will become your happiness and his sadness also yours. You will become used to hearing your laugh every day, as you dance together in your underwear, build blanket forts on snow days, race each other to the car door. He will laugh in the evening when your hunger makes you irrational. He will make you coffee in bed and declare his plans to experiment the perfect cup of coffee with you. You will learn to appreciate delicately extracted coffee too. He will even become a cat person for you.

Time will pass beyond your awareness. Hours will go by sitting on the roof, lying in bed, driving through fog, listening to music. He will twirl your hair in his fingers and you will feel that tingling from your scalp into your chest every time that makes your world slow down.

He will embrace you in his eyes. His eyes – the ones which open toward you as you both awake. On your left side facing him, you will drift into them; one at a time, your tired focus blurring as your cheek sinks further into your pillow. Blink.

Your *komorebi*. Filtering the day to come from the still of the present.

Blink. A corona of golden yellow, contracting around his pupils as they adjust to the morning brightness, intertwining with a green you only recognize from nature. A forest, as light refracts through gossamer leaves into crisp, damp air. You will study them, engrain them into your mind, adorn your apartment with their color palette.

You will fall in love with his mind.
He will fall in love with yours.
A secret language between only you: organic, wordless,
spoken through the widening and softening of your eyelids,
the movement of his gaze,
his eyebrows,
the pout of his lips,
the posture of your shoulders,
the fidgeting of your fingers.

He knows and you know.

Your morning ritual will often be the only grip the day holds on you to drag you out of bed. Over time, it will develop a choreographed dance - you cooking oatmeal, him reaching over you to grab the coffee spoon, the cats weaving between your feet, energized by their scarfed away breakfast, atop the counter and back down again.

He will pour the coffee. First yours then his. Agave follows, a little in both mugs. He swears you corrupted him with your agave addiction. The glass carafe becomes the centerpiece, the steam rolling upwards in a dance between the rays of light of the rising sun. You will try to block the sun from his eyes, straining your neck upwards, swaying to each side to match his movements.

"Happy breakfast," he will say, holding his fork up. You will untangle your limbs from within your oversized shirt to meet it with your spoon. Your ceremonial clink.

His gaze drops intently toward your coffee mug, followed by a nudge of his brow as he meets your eyes again. No blinking. The completeness of his eye contact will never grow old.

A linear plane across air,

a collision of perception.

You sip. The steam swirls onto your cheeks.

An acidic attack on the roof of your mouth. Sharp. Your lips inadvertently tighten as it purls around your tongue, but his anticipatory fixation on you reverberates laughter through your body so you swallow fast. Your soft smile emerges as your amusement travels upward and outward through the creases framing your eyes.

He sighs, his shoulders slumping. "It's too acidic." Pretending to feel defeated, he stirs more agave in as you promise him the coffee is delicious.

You will see him on the phone, facing the mountains, a silhouette of light will outline his edges and you will hope you never forget his structure.

You will go through life with him.
He will be your best friend, your supporter.
You will be his champion.

He will tell you no one has ever made him feel better so effortlessly. But you will know in that moment that you have never loved someone so effortlessly.

And, as the night ends those days when the incessant motion of life leaves you tense, weighed down on your mattress, exhausted and anxious, he will stroke your forehead between your eyes, down onto the bridge of your nose. Meditative. A rhythm synchronized with the expansion and deflation of your lungs. Your heart slows and your thoughts lull. His comfort becomes your home.

You will grow to love your body and he will show you why it should be loved. He will touch you and it will be gentle.

Intimacy will become safe again.
Each of his kisses cushioned with sincerity.
His hands on your waist,
equanimous, dedicated,
reminding you of the balance between you
        rather than power over you.

But, when you cannot love yourself. As the past infiltrates the present, unwelcomed, unannounced. When the lump in your throat prevents swallowing, constricts air, eliminates voice. When the toes below you no longer tap, your eyes weighed down by your cheeks below. When you sink, unphased by the sun, or the phases of the moon, or the sweet smell of his skin. When you wish to detach yourself from self – a leaf's descent – your past from future, present from dark. When your mind convinces you that you cannot bear the weight of each coming moon, he will hold you upright. You will cry to him and he will cry with you. He will bring you water and take you outside. He will promise to make your life easier and it will be easier. Sleeping will be easier. Smiling will become genuine. Your heart will open and your eyes will open and you will know what it means to love. He will tell you that he knows he just has to water you and give you sunlight.

You're like a plant, he says.

TWENTY NINE

Effortless

Easy.
It will be fluid, comfortable.
It will be the feeling of balance, of rightness.
With him it will be easy.

Your body, on your side, intertwined perfectly in the nooks of his.
Comfort.
Your conversations will stop time.
Engrossed in his voice, in his mind, prying him to speak more—
Speak—
Lean your back against a tree.
Next to him. Fluid.

Your thoughts will spin rapidly.
At the front of your forehead
At the base of your skull

Dizzying and racing

He will know from your eyes.
What are you thinking about? You will tell him.
Balance.

You will miss Liz.

"It will feel effortless." She was right.

THIRTY

The Art of Getting Comfortable In Bed

Pillows. Properly fluffed and smooshed, a large one insulating the window, two in the corner by him tucked under his neck and another behind your shoulders.

Head. Resting on his chest at the perfect angle to receive a kiss as you drift into your first hypnagogic state of the night.

Fan. On, angled down at his side of the bed. His one foot peeking out of comforter, toes hanging over the too-small bed you share.

Your legs. One straight, one habitually bent in a perpendicular angle. Your thigh on his thigh, your calf nestled seamlessly in between his knees. Your arctic toes defrosting under his permanently tropical body.

His arm. Reaching for your shoulder that has twisted its way towards his body. His fingertips, softer than oxalis leaves, making orbits on your skin.

And, your arm. Draped in the cadence of his slow-breathing side, taking note of the way his heart beat emerges across his ribs as they expand.

Deep breaths. A warmth beyond thermal perception, instead released within the absence of inhibition or fear, the ethereal sureness of safety.

THIRTY ONE

Stopped Time

No greater relaxation
Than to stop the
Passage of time

The cars below our window
Halt
The new quiet illuminates
How great the roar of traffic
Was

To be busy is to be loud

The flame stands
upright
Above the wick

The tick of the clock
The one that consumes
All thoughts from my brain at night
Ceases

The fans once straining to cool our skin
No longer flip the corner of the crossword off
The table
    we have been working on that puzzle far too long

No greater relaxation
Than to stop the
Passage of time

A moment of nothingness
With you

The only movement now-
The expansion of your pupils

Your eyes
The quintessential forest
A natural, uninhibited world
Reflected in the iris
Of your seeing me

THIRTY TWO

Currently

My thoughts have leaked from my brain like the lavender scent of my oil diffuser. The issue being that I came to this coffee shop to force ideas out of my head, not into a vapor, but into a tangible experience. Into words. Into images.

My mind is empty but it races. A constant stream of consciousness.

The Man sitting next to me continues to glance over to read what I've written. He might consider these ideas. My perfectionism, however, disagrees.

The water in the clear bottle on the shared table where I work vibrates with the movement of the ideas of others, coming out of their minds onto their pages. The more ideas, the more furiously it vibrates.

The man in the purple shirt who walks in, cringes under the weight of the silence he encounters in this coffee shop.

Ideas are silent. Silence is not scary, it is full.

And The Man next to me peeks again. What do you think of my writing, sir?

The ice in my coffee reminds me of the time passing as the surface of each cube melts. Diluting my caffeine, I tell myself, I'll take a sip before it dilutes away. I take a gulp.

Is it socially acceptable to have my shoes off right now in public? My left toes, squished and suffocated under my right thigh, have become numb. The tingles slowly climb up my foot, sacrificed for the comfort of the rest of my body.

My vagina itches too. I'll itch that

My therapist told me this week that brains are busy. We have hundreds of thoughts, many contradicting. Many automatic. 92% of them are the same as yesterday. So where is my 8%? And why is my memory of yesterday blanketed by an opaque fog. And the more yesterday I try to think back, yesterday's yesterday, and yesterday's yesterday's yesterday, the thicker the fog becomes. I'll remember to ask my therapist next week.

How can I learn with a fog over my past? What must I do to absorb the humid air condensing in my mind?

Dehumidifiers exist. I'll make one for my brain. It will require patience. With myself, with those around me, with my busy schedule, with my life. My therapist tries to make me become gentle with myself. I'll try that. Imperfect ideas are still ideas. I am simply unfinished.

The Man To My Left looks again. Do you have any advice, sir?

I'll clear my lungs with fresh air from the mountains. I'll bring my body to higher heights, to the chiropractor, and back up to the sky. I'll show myself what I can do and I'll prove to myself that I can be who I desire. I'll replace any maladaptive feelings in my heart – those of flashbacks, those of doubts, of self-critiques – with love for life, for myself, for the birds, for the tiny bugs that litter the ground. I'll gaze at the leaves supported by thin stems and wonder how they defy gravity so easily. I'll learn from the birds that fly for the act itself and not an audience. I'll encompass the determination of wildflowers that sprout between harsh cracks in our urbanicity. I'll grow beyond my routine, beyond myself, and beyond what I believe I should be. I'll hum when I feel the need, I'll take off my shoes when I want. I will use my voice.

And when I cannot, when I do not have energy to motivate myself to grow or to even sustain, when I feel the heat behind my eyes as I debate with myself if I'm going to let those tears fall or not. When I do have bad thoughts, and dark images, haunting flashbacks, when I want to pinch my skin and critique my own flesh, as I look in the mirror and feel hatred, I'll set those tears free. I'll put on an oversized t-shirt and I'll let myself feel. I'll let the fog grow for a bit, knowing that tomorrow, I can face the sun even longer than this time. Because I've done it before, and I did it yesterday, and two yesterdays ago, and I'll do it next week, and every year that I live.

72

Because, even with zero ideas, I continue to live.

My consciousness charges on.
My mind will take me infinite places.
My voice is my power.

And, yours is too.

I used to shrink at the sound of birds.
They didn't sound like me
or look like me.
They were creatures:
easily unnoticed,
should be avoided.

Forgive me.
I was cruel,
even in solitude
among the trees and flowers and rocks that demand my attention,
it's the birds that humbly exist.
They soar,
aligned with the clouds,
a lightness I envy.
Here, they sing to an empty audience.
A grace in nature with no reward.

Following the wind
free
burdenless.
A quiet magnificence.
My whistles will never compare;
my selfishness unseen in them.

I shall try to exist with such clarity.

Shifting

Dear reader,

Kirby asked me to write a closing thought for *Sunflowers*. She wanted readers to know where she is now, beyond the narrative you just read. I felt it was important to explain, from my eyes, how Kirby has arrived at the place she is now.

I remember being a young girl playing imaginary games upstairs with Kirby and Sara. We iterated through different personalities, genders, moods; you name it we probably played it.

For the most part, we thrived in these imaginary scenarios - temporarily fusing our brains as we agreed on the progression of the game. We shifted seamlessly through different costumes and hairstyles. We turned hula hoops into office spaces and flannel shirts into skirts.

In this imaginary space, three became one.

We would leave playtime and return to our "real" lives, one becoming three.

We embarked on the daily things of childhood - riding bikes, reading, eating snacks.

Early on, however, I could see darkness hovering around me. I struggled to mask this understanding of darkness.

I remember my first panic attack at five years old, shaking in the shower as I wondered why I existed. Who would create someone so imperfect? Who would create someone as sad as me?

Always in sync, Kirby too could sense the frills of darkness entering our shared room. The darkness invited me in as a friend, allowing me to leave once in a while.

For some reason, the darkness forced its way into Kirby. No offer of friendship, it demanded she make a home within it. There was no option for her to leave.

I observed what was happening, but felt I could do nothing but watch.

One day, young Kirby announced she was going to suffocate herself under a blanket. Sara and I responded fearfully, "no!" You can't suffocate yourself because then you would die, we explained!

Kirby was upset we did not let her suffocate, though she did not want to die. We never told Mom.

We never discussed what happened.

I remember sitting in the Whole Foods parking lot with Kirby as she sobbingly described what really happened to her the first week of college. We cried together as we struggled to comprehend the evil that, like the darkness of our childhood, had forced its way into her life.

We were interrupted by a misdirected phone call from my mom and I hung up the phone in rage.

Thus began a long process of breaking, piece by piece.

I observed what was happening, but felt I could do nothing.

I would observe Kirby reaching out her hand searchingly to find the edges of herself. These edges, when she happened to find them, were at once too much and not enough.

Too big, too small, too curly, too frizzy, too sad.

Not big enough, not smooth enough, not happy enough.

These tensions have tugged at her since we were young.

The desire to suffocate, but not to die.

And yet, I see Kirby now, two years into her intensive process of healing, no longer at war with her edges.

Truthfully, I think she now sometimes has trouble finding where she ends (because there is no end).

She is an unstoppable bloom is in progress.

Kirby has endured levels of suffering beyond many people's imagination. Yet, her heart is endless.

Thus continues a long process of healing, piece by piece.

Despite all, a steadying thread throughout my life has always been Kirby. Kirby, who, as a kid, would let me sleep with her in bed when I was too anxious to close my eyes at night (with her, I would fall asleep immediately). The only person who understands my silence and how lost I become when I enter the depths of my brain.

Kirby, who despite often feeling tortured on the inside, cares about everybody else's well-being first.

The book you hold now is a big part of why Kirby has finally shifted to find a home within herself. What started off as a class essay has turned into a transformative work of art. What at first felt like a life-shattering trauma, is now integrated as part of her story.

She has shifted to now regard eating as a part of life and not an evil she must overcome. She has learned to rejoice in herself and I see that she laughs from her stomach - allowing her piercing blue eyes to crinkle. She has learned to love her curly hair instead of straightening it into submission.

Most importantly, Kirby has learned that she can be dark and light at the same time.

Reader: know that there is a resiliency inside of Kirby that will never be shattered. There is no end to what she is capable of. Thank you for celebrating her journey.

Kirby: all that you are has always been exactly as it should be.

Your parallel,
Katharyn

SUNFLOWERS

KIRBY PETERMAN

#LoveLikeNicky

KIRBY PETERMAN

Thank you...

Parul Bavishi (@publishinguncovered) - My editor and supporter. Who encouraged me beyond my doubts.

Mom and Dad - Who I understand now. Thank you for always being my lifeline. I love you both.

To all women and men who have survived sexual assault or sexual harassment.

I stand with you as you learn to share your voice.

KIRBY PETERMAN

About the author...

Kirby Peterman is a Houston, Texas native. She received her BA in Neuroscience and Psychology from the University of Colorado Boulder and now spends her time working, drawing, and exploring the natural world.

Please feel free to contact Kirby directly if you have anything to share about *Sunflowers*, your experiences, thoughts, or just to talk.
sunflowersbook@gmail.com
Instagram @kirbypeterman

To read more by Kirby, visit kirbypeterman.com

52026375R00049